FUN POEMS & PICTURES FOR SCHOOL KIDS

JIM TEETERS

World Enough
Writers

Poetry
ISBN 978-1-937797-07-2

Cover art by Zoe Hickam

Zoe Hickam photo by Rhionna Watson

Interior art & author photo by Jim Teeters

Book Text and Cover Design by Tonya Namura
using LunchBox Slab (display) and Liberation Serif (text)

World Enough Writers
PO Box 445
Tillamook. OR 97141

http://WorldEnoughWriters.com

WorldEnoughWriters@gmail.com

This book is dedicated to all the many kids over the years who have discovered the poets within them.

I am especially grateful to the kindergarten kids I've worked with who found a way forward to reading and writing by taking a stab at poetry.

Also, I appreciate and admire the teachers I've helped–such hard-working sacrificial souls they are!

TABLE OF CONTENTS

CHILDHOOD TRIALS

SCHOOL
DAYS

HALL PASS

Calvin didn't mean to trip me
on the playground yesterday.
But I got a pass to see the nurse
even though I felt okay.

She looked me up and down,
decided I wouldn't die,
put a bandage on my elbow,
and one above my eye.

I went back to class
and everybody smiled.
I never felt so important.
What a lucky child!

The teacher even hugged me.
She was glad I was okay.
She let me skip the test.
But I had to take it another day!

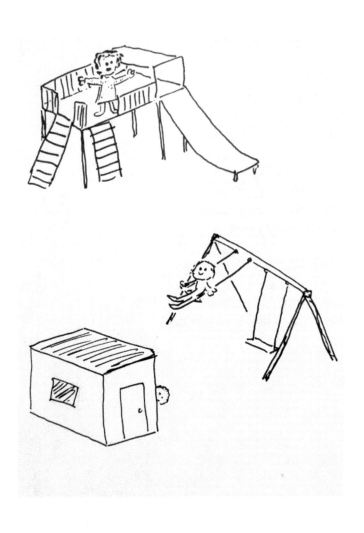

ON THE PLAYGROUND

When you are on the climber
and you climb up and up and up and up,
will you fall!?
...You just twist down the slide and get off
...that's all.

When you are swinging on the swings
and you go higher and higher and higher and higher,
will you fall?
...You just come to a stop and get off
...that's all.

When we are playing hide and seek
and you hide and hide and hide and hide,
will you disappear?
...You soon are by my side
...right here.

When you are climbing, swinging, or hiding
I don't have to fear!

PLAYGROUND RACE

There's this girl on the playground
I decide to race.
So, I go over to challenge her
with a smile on my face.

"Race ya to the swings.
See who'll be the winner."
(She's kind of chubby
and I am much thinner.)

"Okay, on your mark,
ready, set, and GO!"
She starts running fast.
I seem so slow.

We're halfway there.
She starts chuckling.
I'm coughing and spitting,
really white knuckling.

Now she's finished the race.
And I'm coming in last.
I wish I had known
she was so fast.

We hug each other
just to let off steam.
Then she says she's a member
of the track and field team.

RECESS RAIN

The rainfall
left many puddles
on the playground, the other day.
The recess lady told us
we had to stay away.

My friends and I
couldn't help it.
We splashed in them anyway.

We soaked our shoes and socks.
Our pant legs got all wet.
And the playground lady
hadn't even seen us yet.

But then we saw her coming over.
We tried looking innocent and dry.
Our splashing quickly ended.
Now she caught us, we couldn't lie.

The recess lady laughed a little.
Then she told us to go play
in a drier spot.
We just waited for
another rainy day.

THAT RULE

You have to go to school.
You have to go to school.
You have to go to school.
That's a rule.

If I didn't go to school
I'd be breaking that rule.
And someone would
think I'm a fool.

It's learn, learn, learn
each and every day.
Except when we go out
at recess to play.

Class is a bore.
And I hate taking a test.
Though I guess
all grown-ups know best.

So, I'll just go to school
and follow that rule.
And when I'm all grown up,
then I'll take a rest.

THE BULLY

I got sent to the counselor.
Some said I was a bully.
It's true I'd make kids cry
if they didn't suit me fully.

The counselor asked me questions,
but mostly she let me speak.
I talked about my feelings,
where I was strong or I felt weak.

She listens to my parents
and my older brother Fred.
Then I told them how my brother
would always slap me on the head.

I guess he didn't realize
how that would make me mad.
Then I'd take it out on other kids
and that made them sad.

My older brother felt so bad
he cried and he apologized to me.
He said he'd never do it again
and that really set me free.

At class I told each kid I hurt
how sorry that I was,
and about my brother's hitting me,
so, I hit them just because.

Well, I apologized to everyone
and asked forgiveness just last week.
I got lots of hugs and stuff.
One cute girl even kissed me on the cheek.

I learned so much from this.
Here is what I have to say
to any bully who wants to hurt—
Let a good counselor show the way!

THE TEST

Our teacher made us take a test
to see how smart were.
I wasn't really ready.
I was kinda mad at her.

I sat next to another kid.
Thought I'd take a peek,
copied off his answers,
and not get caught a sneak.

Seeing his paper was simple,
as easy as a song,
But when I got my test back,
my answers were all wrong.

So, here's the moral—
Now what's done is done.
If you peek at some kid's paper,
sit next to a smarter one.

DOGS, BUGS &
AN OLD LADY

BEWARE OF DOG

Beware
  of dog.

Be *aware*
  of dog.

Be *wary*
  of dog.

Don't be *where*
  the dog *is.*

Be *where*
  the dog is *not.*

Beware
  of *cat...*
I'll end with that!

CHICO

My mom's voice is shrill.
"Wake up, time to go!
The men are here
to move our trailer."

I ask, "Where's Chico?"

"Don't bother me
about your dog," she snarls.

I get dressed, go hunting,
call into the night:
"CHICO, CHICO!"
My faithful dog,
now lost in the dark,
my heart full of fright.
"CHICO, CHICO!"

"Get in the truck, NOW!"
My dad grabs my hand.

One last plea: "CHICO, CHICO!"
Then, paws on my knee!
Chico!

FLY

While sitting on the steps,
a fly landed on my finger.
I kept very still
and wondered
what made it linger?

Then it landed on my nose
and I swatted it away.
Do you think that little fly
wanted me to play?

Next it flew around my head,
then landed on my knee.
It rubbed its little feet and
danced around happily.

I just knew this couldn't last,
a friendship with a fly?
And soon it went flitting off.
I bid it a sad goodbye.

The next time I saw a fly
land on my window sill,
I didn't swat it, NO!
Just opened up the window,
bid it a fond farewell.

OLD LADY LIVED IN A BOX

There was an old lady
who lived in a box.
She was never on time
though she had lots of clocks.

She was late to church.
She was late to work.
If she came on time,
it gave people shocks.

No one knew
'til it came out one day
why she was late
from her box with the clocks.

Though the box opened wide,
she just couldn't decide
which to put on her feet first,
her shoes or her socks.

SPIDER IN MY BATHTUB

This morning when I got up,
in our bathtub was a spider.
It was huge and black
and made me kind of shudder.

My dad was off at work,
so I yelled for my mother.
She just shrieked and said
she didn't want to bother.

It was up to me I guess.
I thought about it hard.
Then I went to get a jar
and an old used postcard.

I sneaked up on it,
covered it with the jar.
It scrambled up and down
but it couldn't get very far.

I slipped the postcard underneath
as if it were a lid,
looked it in its many eyes.
I was the bravest kid.

I carried it through the back door,
let it loose out by a tree.
And I do believe that spider
waved back thankfully at me.

UNU WAS A FROZEN DOG...

Who came alive after he thawed.
Came alive and barked again!
His hair fell out.
Just bone and skin.

Unu trotted off to town,
fell in a creek and almost drowned.
Wandered the streets wet and cold,
and begged for food.
So I was told.

One small girl with one big heart
wheeled him home in a grocery cart
"No dogs please," said her old man.
Unu's out in
the garbage can.

Now he lives by an old shack.
He guards the place and lives off scraps.
Stays up late and howls at stars.
Sings to the moon
and barks at cars.

Unu thinks about his fate
as he howls, barks, and stays up late.
It could be worse, this is true.
If you were him,
what would you do?

WISHES & WANTS

CHILDREN IN MANY LANDS

Children like to play
games, yes, and much more.
Running to nowhere.
Jumping for no reason.
Moving, laughing, turning, twisting, skipping.
Dreaming!

Some are forced to work.
Girls carry water jugs on their heads.
Boys tend cattle.
But playing is on their minds,
praying for a chance.

Learning, yes.
School, yes.
And learn they do.
But all the time,
waiting to play,
wanting to play.

I AM A MONSTER

I am a monster.
My skin is all green.
I look in a mirror,
even I want to scream.

I am a monster.
But I'm not very big.
Watch where you step,
I'm small as a twig.

I am a monster
with dark scary eyes.
I creep around your house
but just swallow flies.

Although I'm a monster,
I can't scare a soul.
I just eat flies
with milk in a bowl.

I LOVE TO GET PRESENTS

I love to get
presents.
    How about you?
I want something fun,
    not a shoe.
I want something yummy,
    not a bottle of glue,
We want something exciting,
    isn't that true?

Give me an airplane,
    give me some candy.
Maybe a pony.
    Wouldn't that be dandy?
Give me a puppy,
    better yet a little baby lamb.
Then I'd be as
    happy as a clam!

IF I WERE SUPER!

If I were super boy or girl
I would fly, I would twirl.

I would grab you up,
fly you all around
just to see how high
above the ground you'd go
before you'd scream.

Then I would gently
set you down,
fly out and buy us
some ice cream.

THE PUPPY

I want it.
  I want it.
    I want it so much.
I really must have it.
  To look at and touch.
I asked Santa Claus.
  And my parents too.
I begged and I pleaded
  for my wish to come true.

I tried to be good.
  Even said a prayer.
I gave up all hope...
  but soon it was there!
Oh, thank you.
  Oh, thank you.
I yelled, "Oh, yahoo!"
  I hugged it and kissed it.
    And it kissed me back too.

TAKE ME

Take me to the movies.
Take me to the show.
Take me to get ice cream.
Take me to the snow.

Take me to your leader.
Take me to a zoo.
Take me to the ocean.
Take me to buy glue.

Take me to the forest.
Take me up a hill.
Take me to Alaska.
Take me to Brazil.

Take me somewhere dangerous,
where I'll freeze with mortal fear.
Take me, take me anywhere.
I'm sick and tired of being here!

CHILDHOOD
TRIALS

CAN'T SLEEP

At night when I go to bed,
my eyes closed tight,
no tummy ache,
I think of nothing.
But somehow
I lay awake.

Perhaps it's how dark it is.
No longer bright,
I start to shake.
I reach for the lamp switch.
Change my mind.
I start to quake.

Then, I think of my family,
though out of sight,
and I no longer shake.
I close my eyes again,
start to dream.
We're at the lake!

MY TOOTH

for Ellen, 3rd Grade

I have nice teeth.
But one came out.
I cried a little,
but didn't shout.

I took my tooth
to show and tell.
Some kids giggled,
but none yelled.

My teacher looked
it up and down.
She didn't laugh,
but didn't frown.

I put the tooth
beneath my head.
A dime appeared
upon my bed.

My tooth was taken
to who knows where?
Luckily,
I have a spare.

LEARNING TO SWIM

It's scary learning to swim.
Cold water swallows me.
I shiver and shake.
Shake and shiver
in this cold river.

But I will try once again.
Head up, chest out,
I shiver and shake.
Shake and shiver.
But I am swimming
in this cold river!

LONELY

Sometimes I feel so lonely,
even though I'm not alone.
Kids are all around me,
but they treat me like a stone.
No one wants to talk to me
or asks me to play a game.
I stand here drearily
sort of feeling really lame.
Then I see another kid
standing all alone like me.
I get brave, go over.
Soon we're playing happily.

WAITING

I wait in the lunch line.
At recess I wait to swing.
I wait for the school bus, too.
Seems I wait for everything.

I hate waiting at the dentist.
And when I open wide
will she poke me with a needle?
If so, I'll run and hide.

I even wait at home.
when I'm waiting to be fed.
But one thing I CAN wait for
is waiting to go to bed!

BIRD OF MY HEART

The bird of my heart
flutters
away.

The wings of my soul,
drooping
today.

Another day like
any other.
I'll have to go and
tell my mother.

She will hold me
on her loving lap
and my little wings
will start to flap.

ABOUT THE COVER ARTIST

Zoe Hickam is a Seattle-based artist who loves to paint.
Her day job is a massage therapist, but art is her other
love. She enjoys hiking and spending time with her
husband and their dogs.

ABOUT THE AUTHOR

Jim Teeters has written nine poetry collections. He encourages kids to write poetry through his booth "My Goldfish Stole the Moon: Poetry Fun!" at special event and fairs. He volunteers in public schools, working with kids, but also encourages elders to write as coordinator of Ye Olde Poetry Corner at the City of Kent Senior Center in Kent, Washington. Jim also conducts poetry writing sessions at a local homeless women's shelter. He is often referred to as "the poet guy."

CPSIA information can be obtained
at www.ICGtesting.com
Printed in the USA
FFHW02n0504151018
48777081-52893FF